For Maeve Parser

A COMICK BOOK
OF SPORTS

A COMICK BOOK of SPORTS

CLEAN MIND

CLEAN BODY

TAKE YOUR CHOICE

THOUGHT UP, WRITTEN, DRAWN & FOISTED ON AN UNSUSPECTING PUBLIC BY

ARNOLD ROTH

Charles Scribner's Sons, New York

...for my brother Walter...
who started this mess.

1 3 5 7 9 11 13 15 17 19 RD/C 20 18 16 14 12 10 8 6 4 2

Printed in the United States of America
Library of Congress Catalog Card Number 73-1379
ISBN 0-684-13886-7 (RB)

Table of Contents

SPORTS

For the longest time there were no SPORTS.
Mostly because there were no PEOPLE . . .
as this picture proves.

The next day, a caveman named Abner Doublesmqk picked up a ROCK which he didn't need or know what to do with.

So, he threw the rock away and SPORTS were invented.

Some religious scholars have a different THEORY on how sports started and their guess is as good as ours.

Some people think Galileo invented sports.

Some people think Galileo invented everything.

On some other day, someone invented WORK . . .

. . . and everything left over was given rules, regulations, equipment and called SPORTS.

There are sports for INDIVIDUALS

and there are TEAM sports.

AMATEUR athletes play for LOVE.

An obvious AMATEUR.

PROFESSIONAL athletes play for love and MONEY.

A real PRO.

OWNERS of professional teams don't play but love money.

His OWN man.

Teams are often named after ANIMALS . . .

. . . or RACES . . .

. . . or SCHOOLS . . .

. . . or PLACES . . .

. . . or ANYTHING.

Some games are played to a clock.

Some are measured by distance.

Some have equal turns.

Some go their own way.

People who follow or attend sports events are called FANS ... which is short for FANATICS.

A DEDICATED FAN in the OFF SEASON!

Sports make life richer and more exciting, so there!

SPORTS IMPROVING REAL LIFE.

Many people say
Abner Doubleday
invented baseball.

But then again,
many people say
anything that comes
to mind.

A recognizable form of baseball
was played in England during the MIDDLE AGES.

It didn't become popular then because
they kept running out of PITCHERS.

The closest ancestor of baseball was an eighteenth-century
English game called ROUNDERS.

In spite of that,
baseball seems to have
been invented in 1845 by
a New York City volunteer
fireman named Alexander
Joy Cartwright.

People who still want to
believe in Abner
Doubleday probably think
the two-base hit is
named after him.

The purpose in baseball is to score more RUNS than the other team.
A run is scored each time a BASE RUNNER crosses HOME PLATE safely.

Each team is AT BAT until
it makes THREE OUTS
in an INNING.

Baseball is not played to a clock.
A regulation game is NINE innings.

The same players play both
OFFENSE (batting) and DEFENSE
(fielding).

Because of its shape,
a baseball field is sometimes
called a DIAMOND.

BASIC EQUIPMENT

18

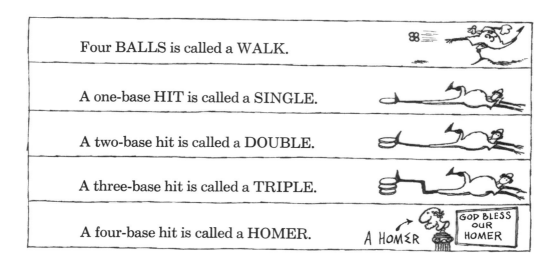

Four BALLS is called a WALK.

A one-base HIT is called a SINGLE.

A two-base hit is called a DOUBLE.

A three-base hit is called a TRIPLE.

A four-base hit is called a HOMER.

A HOMER

GOD BLESS
OUR
HOMER

UMPIRE'S SIGNALS

SAFE

OUT

BALL

UNFAIR   How true!

STRIKE

A team consists of nine players and a MANAGER who is in charge of thinking and INSPIRATION.

Hit homers!
Pitch no-hitters!
Smack bingles!

Yes, mentor!   Amentor!

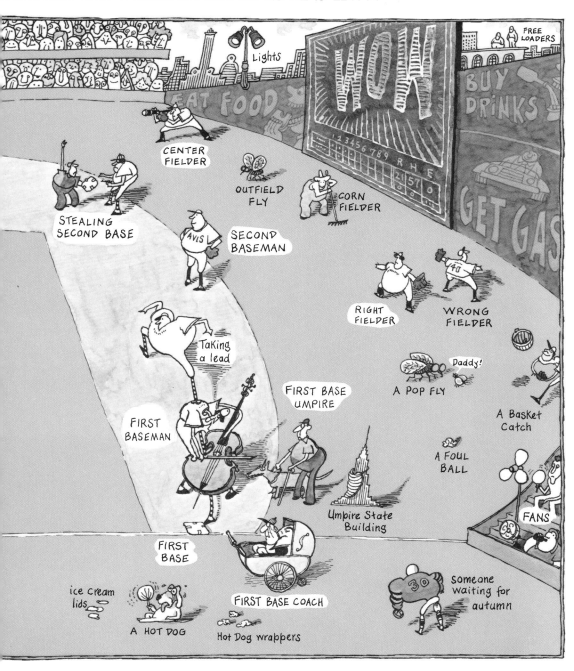

HOW TO PLAY BASEBALL

FIELDING THE FLY BALL

FIELDING THE GROUND BALL

HOW TO BAT

HOW TO SLIDE

HOW TO PITCH

Hide ball behind your back... approve signal from catcher.	Lean forward.	Rear back.	Lift your leg.
Stretch arms.	Lift other leg.	Fall down...	...and make a fool of yourself. I want my mommy!
Throw ball toward home plate.	Hope and pray. KERACK	Keep your eye on the ball... WHOOSH	...and wash behind your ears! SHOWERS

BASEBALL QUIZ
(answer TRUE, FALSE or NO OPINION)

1.	A baseball is sometimes called a HORSEHIDE because of its cover?
2.	Because of the wood it's made from, the bat is sometimes called a HICKORY?
3.	Umpires, because of their decisions, are sometimes called ⊚☆!!✻?
4.	Sometimes, on account of rain, a game is called?
5.	Because of the questions in it, this quiz is called STUPID?

ANSWERS: All are TRUE except number 5 which is NO OPINION.

23

EARLY RUGBY

EARLY PIGSKIN

The football is OVOID and was designed to be kicked or held. The first PASS play (Moore to Van Tassel, Wesleyan vs. Yale, 1906) changed the game and the football is more tapered now.

I got tired of being kicked around.

a tired football

Football is a CONTACT sport and players must PROTECT themselves.

A typical player.

Shoulder pads, rib pads and hip pads.

Elbow pads, thigh pads, arm pads and knee pads.

Shin pads, heavy socks and cleated shoes.

Jersey and pants.

Helmet and face guard.

Like, what's happenin'?

Ready for action.

OFFENSIVE LINE-UP. ELEVEN PLAYERS. SEVEN in the LINE OF SCRIMMAGE. FOUR in the BACKFIELD.

RUNNING BACK

Two dimes One nickel Hut hut

QUARTERBACK

ANOTHER RUNNING BACK

A VERY WIDE RECEIVER

WIDE RECEIVER — RIGHT TACKLE — RIGHT GUARD — CENTER — LEFT GUARD — BLOCK &TACKLE — TIGHT END — BOOK END

Different SQUADS play OFFENSE (when the team has the ball) and DEFENSE (when their OPPONENTS have the ball).

AN OFFENSIVE SQUAD   A DEFENSIVE SQUAD

A FOOTBALL BOOK OF NUMBERS

A game is 60 minutes long.

There are 2, 30-minute ½'s; 4, 15-minute ¼'s.

Each team fields 11 players at a time.

Each team is allowed 6 time-outs; 3 in each ½.

The field is 100 yards long, 53⅓ yards wide. White stripes cross the field every 5 yards. "Hash marks" mark each yard.

The offensive team has a set of 4 downs (tries) to gain at least 10 yards to get another set of downs (called a first down).

Teams change directions each ¼.

A TOUCHDOWN (crossing opponent's goal) is 6 points.

A CONVERSION (kick through goal posts after touchdown) is 1 point.

A FIELD GOAL (kick through goal posts from scrimmage) is 3 points.

A SAFETY (opponent's ball downed behind his own goal line) is 2 points.

A SINGLE picture is worth 1,000 words.

SOME THINGS TO DO IN FOOTBALL

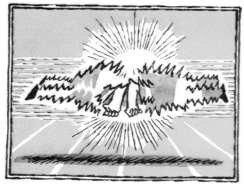

BLOCKING

TACKLING

RUNNING

FUMBLING

PENALTIES

PASSING

HAL

CATCHING

FIRST DOWN

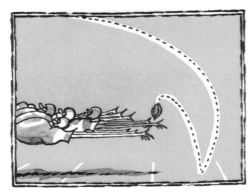

FIRST AID

KICKING

TOUCHDOWN

PRAYING

Dr. NAISMITH inventing BASKETBALL & PEACH JELLY.

Until basketball rules were standardized in 1934, the game was played in many different ways.

There are FIVE on a team: two FORWARDS, two GUARDS and one CENTER.

The object of the
game is to throw
the ball through
the basket. A FIELD
GOAL is worth
two points.

The team with most points when
time runs out is the WINNER.

FOULS are called by the
REFEREES—continually.

One of the most common plays is FOUL SHOOTING
since almost everything anyone does is a foul.

 Basketball players should be tall so as to be closer to the basket.

BASIC PLAYS:

PASSING

SHOOTING

DRIBBLING

DEFENSE

The main purpose of the DEFENDER is to keep
the opposition from SCORING.

THREE DEFENSIVE MOVES:

1. Block vision of basket.
2. Influence ball handling.
3. Control footwork.
4. Don't get caught doing any of these.

OTHER DEFENSIVE PLAYS:

Steal the dribble.

Intercept the pass.

Stay with your man.

Get fouled.

Grab the rebound.

OFFENSE

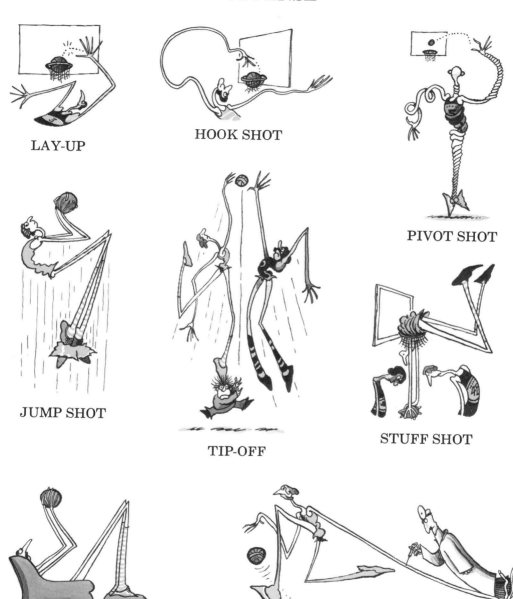

LAY-UP

HOOK SHOT

PIVOT SHOT

JUMP SHOT

TIP-OFF

STUFF SHOT

SET SHOT

FLU SHOT

37

A BASKETBALL PLAY

A MELLOW DRAMA IN TOO MANY ACTS

1. Ball is passed into COURT.

2. Ball is dribbled.

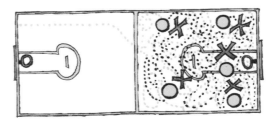

3. It is passed . . . and dribbled . . . and passed . . . and dribbled an awful lot.

4. Someone shoots . . . and misses . . . and gets the rebound . . . and
   shoots . . . and misses . . . and rebounds . . . and shoots . . . and misses.

5. The crowd goes wild.

6. The center stuffs . . . and makes it.

7. The crowd relaxes.

8. Cheers are cheered.

9. Music sounds.

10. And they do it
all over again.

ORGANIZED basketball is played indoors but most
basketball is played in playgrounds, behind
garages and in the streets.

TENNIS & OTHER GAMES PLAYED with RACKETS or PADDLES and NETS

Tennis is a game of GOOD FORM, GOOD MANNERS and BIG WHITE LIES.

Supposedly tennis got its start in France during the AGE OF CHIVALRY and A LOT OF SPARE TIME.

Modern tennis was devised in 1873 by an Englishman, Colonel Walter C. Wingfield, who called it SPHAIRISTIKE and gave the court an hourglass shape.

Today, it is played
all over the world.

ALL OVER THE WORLD

VITAL TENNIS STROKES

FOREHAND   BACKHAND   LOB   SMASH

SERVICE

TENNIS QUIZ	ANSWERS
1. What in the deuce does "deuce" mean?	1. I don't know, either.
2. Is the tennis racket illegal?	2. No! Illegal is a sick bird.
3. Which is larger: tennis or ninenis?	3. Neither.
4. How about elevennis?	4. Both.
5. How do you spell "advantage"?	5. So do I.

BADMINTON is similar to tennis except that a shuttlecock is used instead of a ball, the net is five feet high, the racquet is smaller and the racket is louder.

VERY BAD MINTON

VOLLEYBALL is played by two, nine-member teams. The ball can be hit no more than three times per team, with the hands only, into the air before it must go over the net.

SQUASH uses all surfaces of an enclosed room.

TABLE TENNIS is similar to court tennis except that it is played on a table. Many people call it PING PONG because that's the way it sounds.

LACROSSE is played with netted scoops and a very hard ball. It origina

JAI ALAI is pronounced "HI LI" by people
who know what they're talking about but
don't care how they spell it.

HANDBALL is like squash but a small leather glove is used
instead of a racket.

h American Indians . . . before the cavalry arrived.

THERE ARE TWO KINDS OF HOCKEY: ICE AND FIELD.

Through no fault of the people living there,  ICE HOCKEY did not originate in Africa.

Ice hockey originated in Canada in the nineteenth century...
maybe by someone named Hocque Puhque, though we doubt it.

There are six players on a hockey team:

One CENTER

Two WINGS

Two DEFENSE MEN

One GOALIE

They play on an ice RINK.

Rinks are rimmed by a 4-foot-high fence which deflects pucks.

THE FENCE THAT FAILED

Games are 60 minutes long.

SIXTY MINUTES LONG

A curved hockey STICK is used to hit or shove a hard rubber disk called the PUCK.

HOCKEY STICK

PUCK

They must get the puck into the GOAL to score a point.

A POINT

The team with the most goals wins.

WINNERS

Players who break the RULES are sent into the PENALTY BOX for specific numbers of minutes.

A BROKEN RULE

A PENALTY BOX

FIELD HOCKEY is played on foot with curved sticks and a ball in a field.

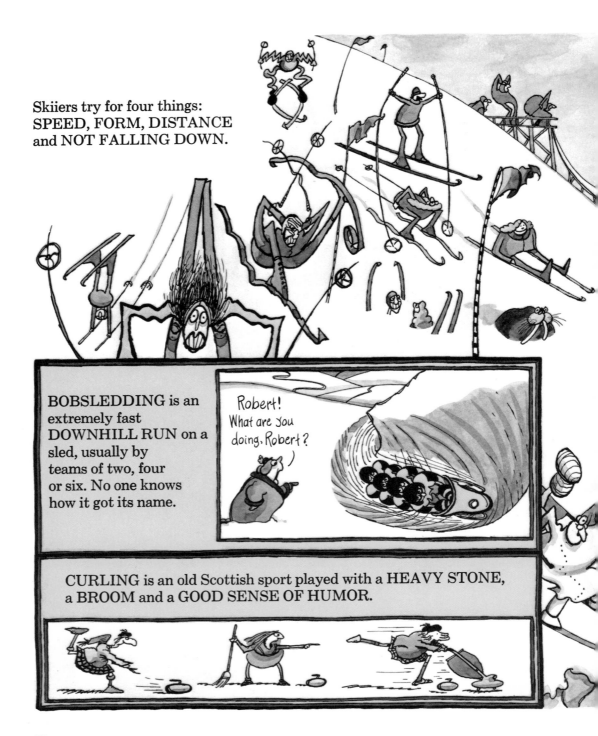

Skiiers try for four things:
SPEED, FORM, DISTANCE
and NOT FALLING DOWN.

BOBSLEDDING is an
extremely fast
DOWNHILL RUN on a
sled, usually by
teams of two, four
or six. No one knows
how it got its name.

Robert!
What are you
doing, Robert?

CURLING is an old Scottish sport played with a HEAVY STONE,
a BROOM and a GOOD SENSE OF HUMOR.

50

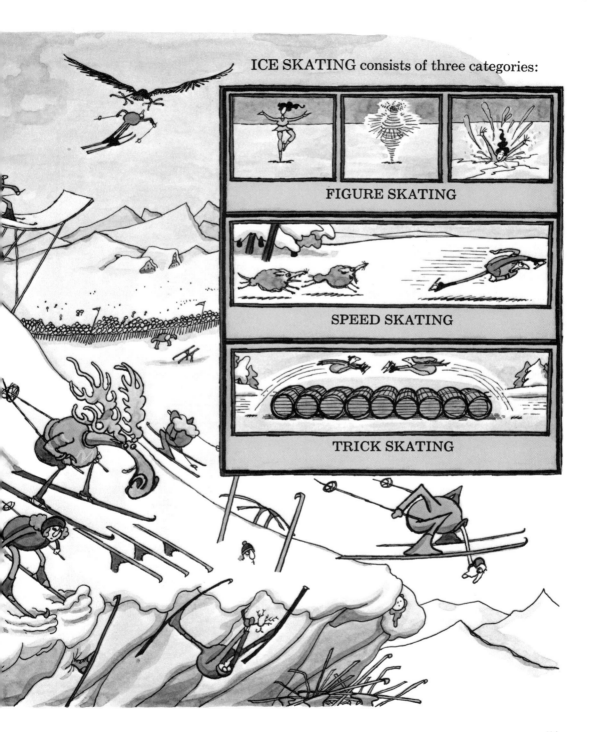

ICE SKATING consists of three categories:

FIGURE SKATING

SPEED SKATING

TRICK SKATING

Golf, like Robert Burns, haggis, tweed, the steam engine and other hot-air makers, got its start in Scotland.

The first golf balls were thin leather covers stuffed with feathers. In 1848 a resin gum ball was adopted. Rubber and plastic balls are used now.

There are three basic shots in golf:

THE DRIVE

THE CHIP (this one from a sand trap)

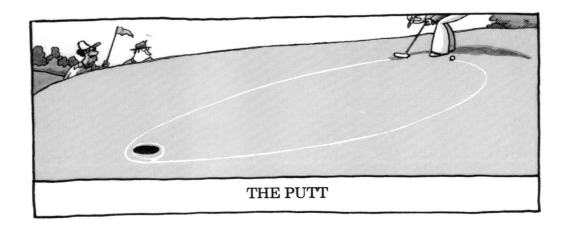

THE PUTT

There are eighteen HOLES to play on a regulation golf course. PAR is the official number of shots it should take to play a hole and/or the course. Numbers of shots are called:

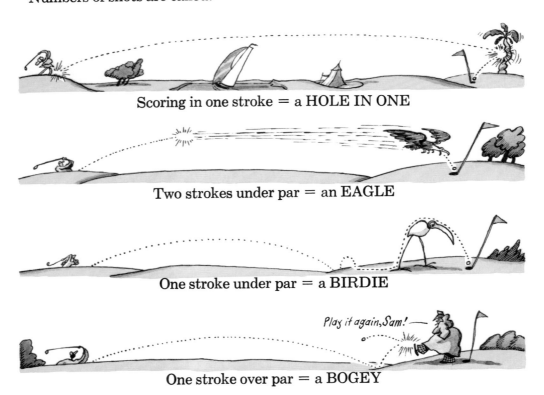

Scoring in one stroke = a HOLE IN ONE

Two strokes under par = an EAGLE

One stroke under par = a BIRDIE

Play it again, Sam!

One stroke over par = a BOGEY

In CROQUET a wooden ball is hit through WICKETS with a wooden MALLET. The game provides opportunities for getting fresh air, doing mean things and hitting your own ankles.

Chicken CROQUET or With Mallets Toward Some

QUOIT players must toss a RING onto a STAKE.

Ha! Missed, again!

HORSESHOE PITCHERS must do the same—but with horses' shoes.

A POCKET BILLIARDS (POOL) ACADEMY AWARD
WINNER: "THE MISSED SHOT"

WATER SPORTS

SURFING! SCUBA! WATER SKIING! WATER POLO! MOTORBOATING!

SWIMMING! DIVING! SAILING! FISHING!

HELP!

There is a theory that the FIRST CREATURES . . .

A FIRST CREATURE

LIVED in the WATER . . .

OLDEN WATER

EMERGED onto LAND . . .

The Land Parts We Watch

then, RETURNED to the WATER!

See? Sure!

Once creature returned to the water, he found two things to do there:

He could SINK . . .

or, he could SWIM.

There are two inspirations for swimming: NECESSITY and SPORT.

A SEEMINGLY NECESSARY SWIM.

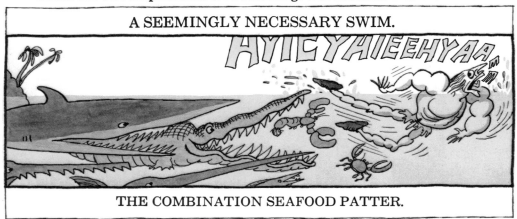

THE COMBINATION SEAFOOD PATTER.

A SPORT SWIM.

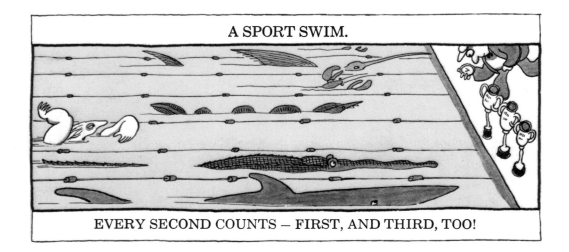

EVERY SECOND COUNTS — FIRST, AND THIRD, TOO!

FAVORITE STROKES

Back Stroke

Breast Stroke

Sun Stroke

Australian Crawl

Dog Paddle

The Float

The Flail

The Drown

· SWIMMING ·

· A GREAT BODY BUILDER ·

59

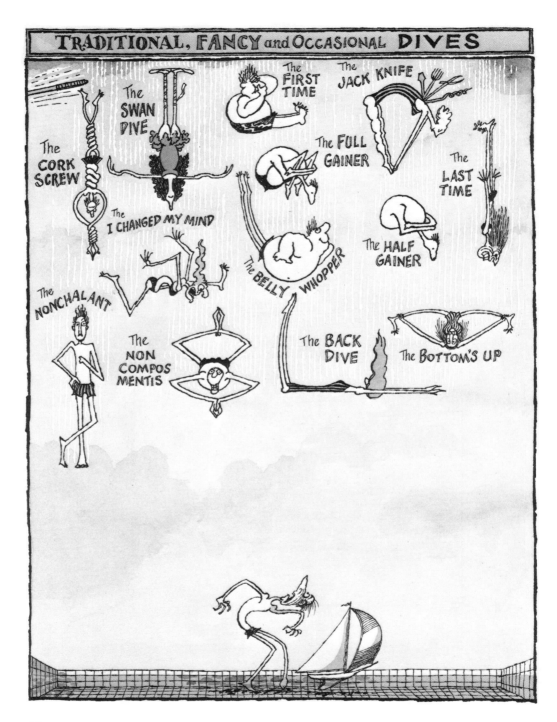

TRADITIONAL, FANCY and OCCASIONAL DIVES

The CORK SCREW

The SWAN DIVE

The I CHANGED MY MIND

The FIRST TIME

The JACK KNIFE

The FULL GAINER

The LAST TIME

The HALF GAINER

The BELLY WHOPPER

The NONCHALANT

The NON COMPOS MENTIS

The BACK DIVE

The BOTTOM'S UP

A WATER SPORT SPECTACULAR: THE SURFER'S ART

WATER SKIING is great for thrills.

WATER POLO is great for action.

SCUBA DIVING is great for meeting other scuba divers.

Since prehistoric times, man has FISHED for food.

Izaak Walton wrote *The Compleat Angler* and popularized fishing as a sport.

Fishing is done in
SALT WATER and
in FRESH WATER.

A FRESH-WATER
FISHERMAN.

A FRESH-WATER FISH.

Fishing from a BOAT.

Fishing from a PEER.

HOW TO CAST A LINE

Hold rod upright.   Swing rod back.   Swing rod forward . . . release catch.

THE FUN OF FISHING EQUIPMENT

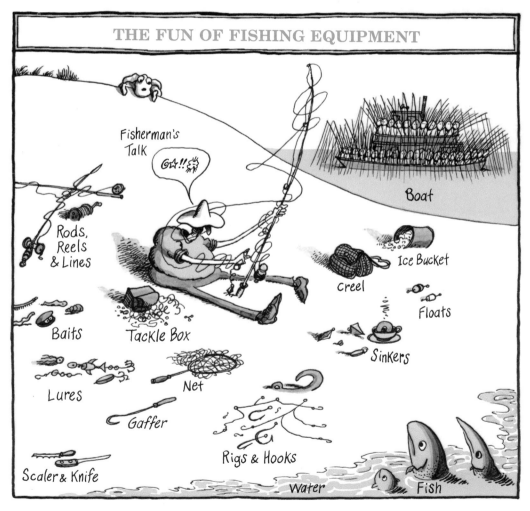

63

MOTORBOATING

TRACK & FIELD

THE LONELINESS OF THE LONG-DISTANCE RUNNER.

In prehistoric times . . . before television was invented . . . a caveman had very few ways to pass the time of day. He could:

In the meantime, the ancient Greeks organized these activities and called them the OLYMPICS as a tribute to their gods' dwelling place.

RUNNING

Short-distance runs are called
SPRINTS or DASHES. Middle- and
long-distance runs are called RUNS.
Running home is not called
a HOME RUN.

Sprinter's starting position.

They're off.

Breasting the tape.

Long-distance running requires PERSEVERANCE, CONDITIONING,
ENDURANCE and a LACK OF SUPERSTITION.

In RELAY races, a runner runs a portion of the distance, then passes a BATON to the next runner on his or her team.

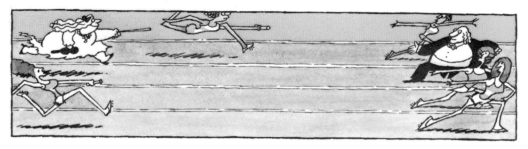

HURDLERS are runners who must jump over equally spaced obstacles called HURDLES. People with mashed potatoes in their mouth should not try to say "hurdles" too often.

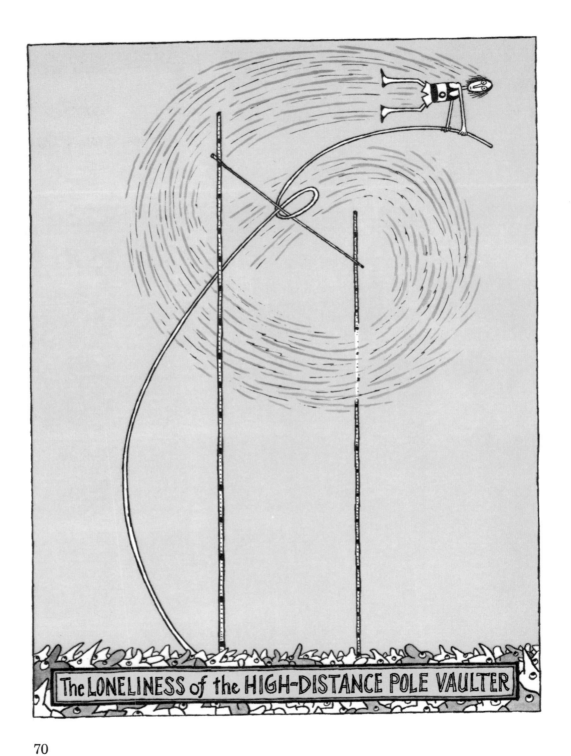

The LONELINESS of the HIGH-DISTANCE POLE VAULTER

THE LONG JUMP

THE HIGH JUMP

THE JAVELIN THROW

THE DISCUS THROW

THE SHOT PUT

 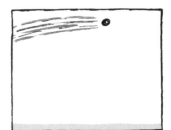 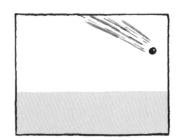

GYMNASTICS

TUMBLING

THE INVENTION

OF TUMBLING

BACK FLIP

SOMERSAULT

WINTER SALT

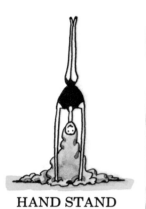

HAND STAND

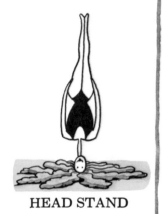

HEAD STAND

HOT DOG STAND

THE HORSE

THE HORIZONTAL BARS

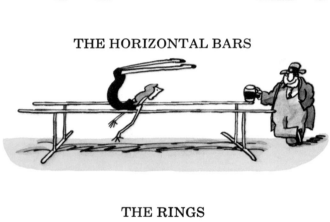

THE RINGS

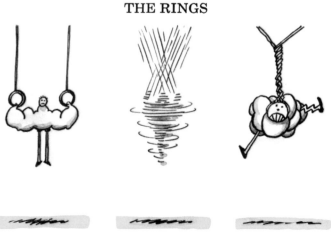

THE GOOD OLD DAYS: BOWLING ON THE GREEN

BOWLERS must knock over as many of the TEN PINS as they can
with no more than two ROLLS.

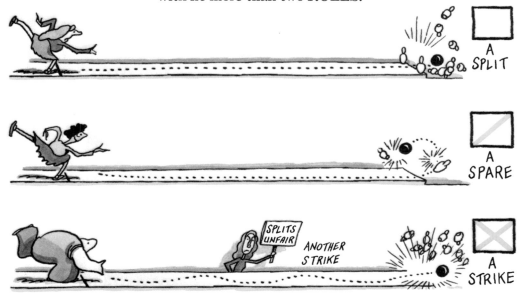

It is wrong to BOUNCE the ball as this oaf is doing.

The ball should be ROLLED as this lady is trying to do.

BOWLING EQUIPMENT

BOWLING BALL   BOWLING PIN   BOWLING SHOES   BOWLER HAT

ARCHERY . . .   . . . TARGET SHOOTING . . .

. . . AND DARTS, ALL REQUIRE . . .

. . . GOOD AIM.

A BOXING FIRST: THE INVENTION OF THE DOUBLE UPPERCUT.

BOXERS are discovered by MANAGERS.

To train, boxers must . . . punch bags . . .  jump rope . . .

do roadwork . . . punch more bags . . . build muscles . . . punch sparring mates . . .

but, if they lose, they must . . .   do more roadwork.

BOXERS ARE CLASSIFIED BY WEIGHT.

A LIGHTWEIGHT   A MIDDLEWEIGHT   A HEAVYWEIGHT

GREAT MOVIE MOMENT: "THE KID'S LAST CHANCE"

WRESTLERS must pin their opponents for a count of THREE.

FENCING

KARATE

THOROUGHBRED RACING

All thoroughbred RACE HORSES are descendants of three
Arabian-English stallions named MATCHEM, HEROD and ECLIPSE.

MATCHEM

HEROD

ECLIPSE

Valuable thoroughbreds are CURRIED and FAVORED in every way.

TRAINING

Before the race,
horses are paraded
in the PADDOCK.

They're in the
STARTING GATE . . .
. . . They're off!

Coming down the
far STRAIGHTAWAY.

A PHOTO FINISH.

The WINNER'S CIRCLE.

HARNESS RACING

Harness horses are either
PACERS or TROTTERS.

A PACER

PACERS move both legs
on the same side
simultaneously
in the same direction.

A TROTTER

TROTTERS simultaneously
move one front leg and the
opposite back leg in
the same direction; and the
other two legs in the
reverse direction.
Trotters must be nuts.

DRIVERS ride in a SULKY.

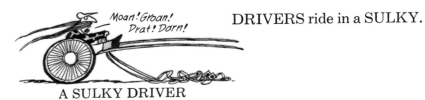

Moan! Groan! Drat! Darn!

A SULKY DRIVER

FANS bet on
their favorites.

FANS

AUTOMOBILE RACING

A DRAG RACE is a quarter-mile straight run with the fastest car winning. Only two cars race at one time.

The drag starts when the bottom light of the countdown "CHRISTMAS TREE" STARTER is lit.

Many DRAGSTERS are slowed by release of a parachute "BRAKE."

In TRACK racing the fastest CAR to cover a given distance wins. With a variety of FLAGS the FLAGMAN STARTS, STOPS, CAUTIONS and CONFUSES the DRIVERS.

Drivers are expert, alert and don't know what DANGER is.

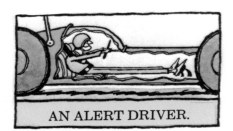

AN ALERT DRIVER.

AN UNALERT DRIVER.

Drivers make PIT STOPS for FUEL, REPAIRS, NEW PARTS, ADVICE, ROAD MAPS and REST ROOMS.

TRACK RACE cars—be they STOCK CARS, MIDGETS or full-size RACERS— must go around an oval track. Occasionally detours arise.

GRAND PRIX ROAD RACING is run on regular STREETS and ROADS in Europe.

THE MEDIEVAL ORIGINS OF SOCCER

Soccer players can HEAD the ball . . .

. . . or KICK the ball . . .

. . . but they cannot propel the ball with their HANDS or ARMS . . . except the GOALIE, who can touch it with anything he wants to.

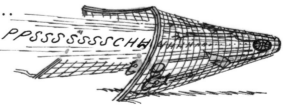

THE DRIBBLE

THE PASS

THE WORLD OF SOCCER

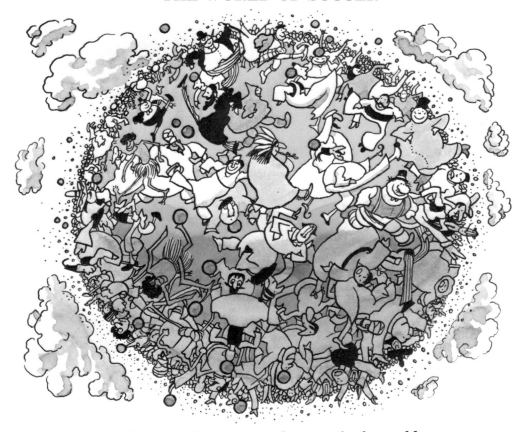

Soccer is the most popular game in the world.

90

91

TIME
HAS
RUN
OUT.